700039032071

The World of
PETER RABBIT
and
BEATRIX POTTER

FREDERICK WARNE

FREDERICK WARNE

Published by the Penguin Group
Penguin Books Ltd., 80 Strand, London WC2R 0RL, England
Penguin Group (USA) Inc., 375 Hudson Street, New York, New York 10014, USA
Penguin Books Australia Ltd., 250 Camberwell Road, Camberwell, Victoria 3124, Australia
Penguin Books Canada Ltd., 90 Eglinton Avenue East, Suite 700, Toronto, Ontario, Canada M4P 2Y3
Penguin Books India (P) Ltd., 11 Community Centre, Panchsheel Park, New Delhi 110017
Penguin Books (NZ) Ltd., 67 Apollo Drive, Rosedale, North Shore 0632, New Zealand
Penguin Books (South Africa) (Pty) Ltd., 24 Sturdee Avenue Rosebank 2196, South Africa

Penguin Books Ltd., Registered Offices: 80 Strand, London WC2R 0RL, England

Website: www.peterrabbit.com

Copyright © Frederick Warne & Co., 2005
This edition published in 2012

001 - 10 9 8 7 6 5 4 3 2 1

Frederick Warne & Co. is the owner of all rights, copyrights and
trademarks in the Beatrix Potter character names and illustrations.

Manufactured in China

ISBN 978-0-7232-6766-9

A VERY

Famous Rabbit

In 1893, a five-year-old child named Noel Moore received a letter that he was to treasure all his life. It told the story of four little rabbits named Flopsy, Mopsy, Cotton-tail and Peter.

PETER RABBIT AND HIS CREATOR

The Tale of Peter Rabbit, telling of Peter's adventures in Mr. McGregor's garden, was to become one of the best-loved stories of all time. Its creator was a young woman with a talent for painting, an acute observational eye and a keen understanding of children – a combination that enabled her to create a collection of animal characters whose popularity endures to this day.

The first part of Beatrix Potter's life was a rather restricted existence, mostly spent with her parents in London, where she created the "little books" that made her famous.

RIGHT: *Beatrix with her father and mother, both pillars of Victorian society.*

The second half was lived in her beloved Lake District where at last she achieved her independence, becoming a successful farmer and passionate conservationist. She always remained surprised by the enduring popularity of Peter Rabbit, but she wrote to a friend, "I often think that was the secret of the success of Peter Rabbit – it was written to a child, not made to order!"

ABOVE: *Beatrix as a young woman of 26.*

A Victorian Childhood

Helen Beatrix Potter was born on 28 July, 1866. Her parents, Rupert and Helen Potter, were affluent and respected members of London society. Beatrix saw little of her parents as a child, being brought up by a nanny and educated at home by a governess. Beatrix's mother did not like her daughter to mix with other children, so Beatrix's brother Bertram, born when she was six, became her chief playmate. The children entertained themselves with reading, drawing, and an extraordinary collection of pets.

LEFT: *Beatrix was very fond of her little brother. This picture was taken in 1878 by their father, Rupert, who was an enthusiastic photographer.*

At various times they had a frog, two lizards, four black newts, a ring-snake, two salamanders, a tortoise and a bat, as well as a succession of rabbits and mice. Together they studied and drew these creatures, which occasionally escaped from the schoolroom and had to be searched for all over the house!

RIGHT: *One of Beatrix's favourite pets was a mouse called Xarifa, whom she often sketched.*

"I THINK SHE WAS IN MANY RESPECTS THE SWEETEST LITTLE ANIMAL I EVER KNEW."

LEFT: *The benefits of Beatrix's early practice sketches show clearly in her later work, such as this picture of country mouse Timmy Willie.*

ANIMAL FRIENDS

Beatrix's favourite animal friends were her pet rabbits. At the beginning of her career she drew many greeting card designs, often using as a model her rabbit, Benjamin Bouncer, or Bounce. His antics were often a source of amusement to the whole family.

When they went on holiday, Benjamin came too, travelling in a little basket. He liked picking and eating gooseberries from bushes. He also had a great fondness for buttered toast and would come running when he heard the tea bell.

BENJAMIN BOUNCER

ABOVE: *Benjamin was a lively bunny, and sometimes attacked visitors!*

When Benjamin died, he was followed by Peter Piper, a Belgian rabbit. Peter had a talent for performing tricks, such as jumping sticks, ringing a bell and banging a tambourine, which made him a favourite with children and a very popular visitor! Beatrix went everywhere with Peter.

ABOVE: *When Benjamin was on holiday in Scotland, Beatrix took him out for walks on a lead to keep him safe from the fierce local cats.*

Above: *Peter Piper as drawn by Beatrix Potter. Peter liked lying right* *front of the fire. Sometimes he even lay inside the fender to get really war*

17

LETTERS TO CHILDREN

As an adult, Beatrix kept in touch with her last governess, Annie Moore, who had left the Potter household to get married and have children. The young Moores looked forward to Beatrix's visits for she sometimes brought her rabbit Peter with her or a basket of white mice. Beatrix was fond of the children too and used to write them illustrated letters telling them all about the antics of Peter Rabbit and other creatures.

ABOVE: *There were eight Moore children, so Beatrix was a busy correspondent.*

ABOVE: *Annie Moore with one of her children.*

BELOW AND LEFT: *The characters from Beatrix's picture letters were often to appear later in books.*

Dec 1st 05.

Dear Winifred,

This is all that is to be seen of Mrs Tiggy today! She went to sleep on Wednesday night and I don't expect her to wake

herself up tighter. When she wakes up she is very lively and dreadfully hungry, and rather wobbly on her legs.

I have been drawing a frog today with a ...

19

THE ORIGINAL PETER RABBIT PICTURE LETTER

In September 1893, while Beatrix was on holiday in Scotland, she heard that Noel, the eldest of the Moore children, was ill. So to cheer him up she sent a letter. It began, "My dear Noel, I don't know what to write to you, so I shall tell you a story about four little rabbits whose names were Flopsy, Mopsy, Cotton-tail and Peter." The letter was full of little pictures and told for the first time the story that was to become popular all over the world as *The Tale of Peter Rabbit*.

RIGHT: *Noel Moore, the first little boy to hear Peter Rabbit's story.*

ABOVE: *Beatrix first told* The Tale of Peter Rabbit *in an eight-page letter full of pen-and-ink drawings.*

RIGHT: *The letter tells how naughty Peter Rabbit goes exploring in Mr. McGregor's garden and only just manages to escape from the angry gardener after an exciting chase.*

'Now, my dears', said old Mrs Bunny 'you may go into the field or down the lane, but don't go into Mr McGregor garden.'

Flopsy, Mopsy & Cottontail, who were good little rabbits went down the lane to gather black berries, but Peter, who was very naughty

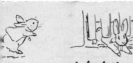

straight away to Mr McGregor's garden
and squeezed underneath the gate.

First he ate some lettuce,
and some broad beans,
then some radishes, and
then, feeling rather sick,
he went to look for
some parsley; but
round the end of a
cucumber frame
whom should he meet but Mr McGregor!

Mr McGregor was planting out young cabbages
but he jumped up & ran after Peter waving
a rake & calling out 'Stop thief'!

Peter was most dreadfully frightened &
rushed all over the garden, for he had
forgotten the way back to the gate.
He lost one of his shoes among the cabbages

and the other shoe amongst the potatoes. After losing them he ran on four legs & went faster, so that I think he would

have got away altogether, if he had not unfortunately run into a gooseberry net and got caught fast by the large buttons on his jacket. It was a blue jacket with brass buttons, quite new.

M.^r McGregor came up with a basket which he intended to pop on the top of Peter, but Peter wriggled out just in time, leaving his jacket behind

and this time he found the gate, slipped underneath and ran home safely.

Mr. McGregor hung up the little jacket & for a scarecrow, to frighten the birds.

was ill during the evening, in consequence eating himself. His mother put him to and gave him a dose of camomile tea,

but Flopsy, Mopsy, and Cottontail had bread and milk and blackberries for supper.   I am coming back to London next Thursday, so I hope I shall see you soon, and the new baby. I remain, dear Noel, yours affectionately
          Beatrix Potter.

25

THE PUBLICATION OF
THE TALE OF PETER RABBIT

Beatrix decided that she wanted to produce a book from her story idea. She sent the Peter Rabbit manuscript to at least six publishers but it was rejected by all of them. So she decided that she would publish it herself. In December 1901 she printed 250 copies which she sold through friends and relations. It did so well that she had to order more.

ABOVE: *Beatrix's own privately-printed edition, illustrated in black and white.*

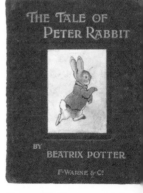

ABOVE: *The first commercial edition, 1902, featuring colour illustrations.*

The book's success encouraged Frederick Warne & Co., one of the firms who had previously rejected the manuscript, to reconsider their decision. They offered to take it on if Beatrix was willing to re-illustrate all her black-line drawings in colour. She agreed. The book was published in October 1902 and it was an immediate bestseller. The book was kept small for "little hands" and sold at the affordable price of five pence.

ABOVE: *Two of Beatrix's colour illustrations for the Frederick Warne edition of* The Tale of Peter Rabbit.

PETER'S COUSIN BENJAMIN

After her initial success with Peter Rabbit, Beatrix focused on different characters for her second and third books, *The Tailor of Gloucester* and *The Tale of Squirrel Nutkin*. But after these she wanted to write a simpler story and decided on a sequel to the Peter Rabbit book in which Peter and his confident cousin Benjamin return to Mr. McGregor's garden and have a very frightening encounter. For all the garden scenes Beatrix used sketches she had made while on holiday at Fawe Park in the Lake District. *The Tale of Benjamin Bunny* was published with great success in 1904.

ABOVE: *A rough sketch of Peter and Benjamin standing on top of the wall.*

ABOVE: *For the book picture Be drew the real wall at Fawe Par*

THE TALE OF BENJAMIN BUNNY

BY BEATRIX POTTER

F. WARNE & C?

LEFT: *First edition (1904)*

BELOW: *Beatrix's painting of Fawe Park garden with its "very fine" lettuces.*

PETER RABBIT'S WORLD

Beatrix liked to imagine her characters in her favourite places, so she created a special world for Peter Rabbit. In 1905 she moved to the Lake District. Its cosy villages and awe-inspiring scenery became the backdrop for many of her later stories, expanding Peter's world and introducing new friends. Many of the locations can still be seen today.

THE FARM

When Beatrix moved to the Lake District, she purchased Hill Top Farm, which is recognisable as the farmhouse inhabited by the cat family – Tom Kitten and his mother and sisters. The rat, Samuel Whiskers, and his wife Anna Maria can also be found there in the attic, although they are not welcome. The farmyard is home to many animals including Jemima Puddle-Duck, Sally Henny-Penny and Kep the sheepdog.

THE WOODS

Although *The Tale of Peter Rabbit* does not have a specific Lake District setting, it is clear from later books that Peter's home is in the woods not far from the village. Other animals who live in the woods include Peter's cousin Benjamin, Squirrel Nutkin, and the untrustworthy foxy-whiskered gentleman – Mr. Tod.

THE HILLSIDE

The Lakeland hills or "fells" are always in the background. Mrs. Tiggy-winkle, the hedgehog washerwoman, has her home behind a secret door on the hillside.

The Village

Everyone goes to the village to shop and gossip. At Ginger and Pickles' shop the customers include Jemima Puddle-Duck, Samuel Whiskers and Peter Rabbit. A rival shop is run by Mrs. Tabitha Twitchit, Tom Kitten's mother.

The Lakes

Lakes are part of the scenery in many tales. Mr. Jeremy Fisher, the frog, lives right beside the water and likes to go fishing in his lily-pad boat.

THE TOWN

Most animals prefer the country but Timmy Willie, the wood-mouse, goes to the town by mistake when he falls asleep in a vegetable hamper. He finds urban life very different...

PETER RABBIT RETURNS

For her third rabbit story, Beatrix decided to tell her readers more about the famous Peter and Benjamin, now grown up. Benjamin has married Peter Rabbit's sister Flopsy, and they have six charming Flopsy Bunnies. Mr. McGregor's garden still provides the tastiest cabbages, but venturing there is as dangerous as ever.

Over the years Mr. McGregor's garden was based on a number of different locations. Peter Rabbit's first foray was set in Scotland. *The Tale of Benjamin Bunny* features Fawe Park in the Lake District; and for the Flopsy Bunnies the setting is a garden in Wales.

ABOVE: *First edition, 1909*

"THE EFFECT OF EATING TOO MUCH LETTUCE IS 'SOPORIFIC'."

ABOVE, BELOW AND RIGHT:
*When Beatrix stayed with her
uncle and aunt in Denbigh, Wales,
she made numerous watercolours
of the garden at Gwaynynog to use
as background scenes.*

Peter Rabbit's Bit Part

Beatrix Potter carried on expanding the world of her early rabbit tales to create a whole community of lovable, if sometimes quarrelsome, imaginary creatures. By this time, Peter Rabbit had become a firm favourite, and he even sneaked into some illustrations in *The Tale of Ginger and Pickles*.

Peter Rabbit is seen heading into Ginger and Pickles' shop with a basket, and later buying from Sally Henny-Penny. Perhaps he has decided that making an honest purchase is safer than seeking the free but dangerous radishes in Mr. McGregor's garden?

ABOVE: *First edition, 1909.*

LEFT: *Peter Rabbit is among the customers of Ginger and Pickles.*

ABOVE: *Peter reads an advertisement for a new rival to Ginger and Pickles.*

LEFT: *Once poor Ginger and Pickles have gone out of business, Peter takes his custom to Sally Henny-Penny.*

Peter Rabbit's Final Tale

In *The Tale of Mr. Tod*, 1912, the Flopsy Bunnies are yet again in danger. Peter and Benjamin set out on a mission to save them and witness a terrible battle between the two enemies Tommy Brock, the badger, and Mr. Tod, the fox.

ABOVE: *First edition, 1912.*

RIGHT: *Illustrations of Mr. Tod and Tommy Brock from* The Tale of Mr. Tod.

This is the last time that Peter Rabbit appeared in one of Beatrix Potter's books. It is a dramatic story and for Beatrix it was a welcome departure from making "books about well-behaved people".

She had a few disagreements with her publishers over the wording, however. She wrote to them, "You are a great deal too much afraid of the public for whom I have never cared one tuppenny-button. I am sure that it is that attitude of mind which has enabled me to keep up the series."

LEFT: *Illustrations from* The Tale of Mr. Tod *with a study of a seated fox (above). The story is set in a real place in the Lake District, Bull Banks.*

PETER MOVES ON

As time went by Beatrix was becoming increasingly involved in the management of her Lake District farms and less interested in her publishing career. But her books were still continuing to sell and there was a growing and successful programme of Peter Rabbit merchandise, which Beatrix herself had started as early as 1903.

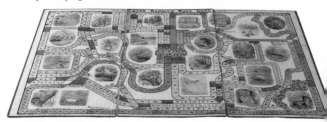

ABOVE: *Beatrix had invented a Peter Rabbit race game for two players in 1904. This more complex version went on sale in 1917.*

LEFT: *Peter Rabbit colouring pages – a set of outlines in an envelope, sold as an addition to* Peter Rabbit's Painting Book.

ABOVE: *Beatrix made and patented the first Peter Rabbit doll in 1903. This is the certificate of registration.*

ABOVE: *The German toy firm Steiff produced Peter Rabbit plush toys under licence with great success from 1904.*

RIGHT: *For the year 1929 Beatrix produced* Peter Rabbit's Almanac.

BEATRIX POTTER'S LEGACY

Beatrix entered old age in good spirits. She took great pleasure in the upkeep of her land and she had accomplished a great deal in her life when she died at the age of 77. She left over 4,000 acres of land to the National Trust, and the incomparable legacy of her books to children everywhere.

LEFT: *Beatrix in 1943 with her two pet Pekingese dogs.*

In the 1930s her publishers had re-issued all her titles in a uniform, small-format series. They included two rhyme books, two reworked concertina books and a final story she had written for her American fans called *The Tale of Little Pig Robinson*. Together these made up the twenty-three "Original Peter Rabbit Books", and that series is still famous throughout the world today.

ABOVE: *Peter Rabbit lives on into the twenty-first century.*

ABOVE: *Modern editions of the twenty-three tales.*

Acknowledgements

The photographs and paintings included in this book are reproduced courtesy of the following:

Page 10 Beatrix with parents, V&A.
Page 11 Beatrix aged 26, V&A.
Page 12 Beatrix and her brother, private collection.
Page 13 Mouse sketch, Linder.
Page 14 Benjamin sketch, Linder.
Page 15 Beatrix with rabbit on lead, private collection.
Pages 16–17 Peter by the fire, Linder.
Page 18 Moore family, Annie Moore, both from private collections.
Page 20 Noel Moore, private collection.
Pages 21–25 The Peter Rabbit Picture Letter, V&A.
Page 28 Rough bunny sketch, V&A.
Page 35 Black-and-white and colour garden sketches without bunnies, both V&A.
Page 39 Fox watercolour, V&A.

All other pictures are from the Warne Archive.